SECRET PLACE *of the* MOST HIGH

A Journal for Those Who Hunger After the Deep Things of God

Jennifer Kennedy Dean

New Hope
Birmingham, Alabama

New Hope
P. O. Box 12065
Birmingham, AL 35202-2065

Dewey Decimal Classification: 248.4
SUBJECT HEADINGS: Spiritual Life
Devotional Exercises

Cover design by Steve Diggs & Friends Advertising/Public Relations

ISBN: 1-56309-204-2

N974110•0397•5M1

"He that dwelleth in the secret place of the most High shall abide under the shadow of the Almighty" (Psalm 91:1 KJV).

GETTING STARTED

Keeping a journal is a discipline that many Christians have found helpful in their spiritual quests. A journal can be a record of your own journey, your own history with God. It can be an effective emotional outlet during times of stress or doubt. Journaling often helps you crystallize your thoughts and see them from a different perspective. You can use your journal to record thoughts or insights or Scriptures God quickens in you. I love to go back through journals and praise God for answers and see how far I've come in my understanding of Him. Some journal entries remind me of instances when I thought everything was hopeless and I couldn't see God anywhere in the picture. Of course, He always came through, but sometimes I have to look back to see His hand. It gives me encouragement for current struggles. I can see a pattern of God's faithfulness.

When a long-term prayer is answered or difficulty is resolved, I am able to look back over my journal entries and see how God has encouraged me and comforted me and challenged me. I can see in my own handwriting when God promised me this very outcome before it existed on the earth. These experiences make it easier to trust His voice.

People journal in a variety of ways. Experiment with journaling methods. One approach may be meaningful one day and another approach more meaningful another day. Let me suggest some possible methods to get you started.

1. You might write out your thoughts as you express them to God. I often journal this way when I need to express confusion or doubt. It helps me pinpoint and define my exact sources of difficulty. I find that it gives me emotional release and also forces me to look at the direction of my thoughts. As I seem to be talking to God, He is really talking to me.

I also journal this way when I am praising Him and when I am exulting in His faithful answer. I write out psalms to Him. Some, I must admit, are more poetic than others; but God is not grading me on my writing ability. He is enjoying my adoration. I have many records of God's workings in my life through this kind of journal entry. Many of these times I have seen God work in a way that no one else would recognize because no one else has been in on our private conversations. If I had not recorded my exultation, I'd have forgotten these incidents.

2. Sometimes one anxious thought piles atop another without my stopping to deal with it until I am loaded down with anxieties I can't even name. David captures this for me in Psalm 94:19 (NASB): "When my anxious thoughts multiply within me," he says. I journal anxiety in two ways.

Sometimes I write down something like: *These are the burdens I am trying to carry. As I write each one down, I am turning it over to You.* Then I list every anxiety. It is freeing because it is such a concrete act. I also find that as I list each anxiety separately, it doesn't look so bad. It's really the whole pile together that weighs me down. At the end of my list, I might write something like: *These are Yours now. Do in them whatever You want. Let Your kingdom come. Let Your will be done.* As time goes by, I go back to my lists of anxious thoughts and make little notes about what God is doing or has done.

Another way that I sometimes deal with anxieties and worries is to write them out in statements of faith. For example, I might write: *I know that nothing is in my life without Your permission. I know that [this situation] is under Your control. I know that nothing is too difficult for You. I know that You have the timing for [this situation] already planned perfectly.* As I write these statements, it looks as if I am making them; but really God is reminding me of His promises and causing me to take hold of them.

3. Sometimes I write out what I sense the Father saying directly to me. I find that as I write, words unfold in my mind and I trust them to be His. Sometimes this is encouragement and promise;

2

other times correction and conviction. Often it is His words of love to me.

4. When I see a pattern of coincidences developing that look like God's hand moving me toward my vision, I write little notes about incidents as they occur. Later, when the vision has taken shape on the earth, I can go back and trace the path. These kinds of journal entries are just phrases with dates beside them.

5. I write out Scripture verses or passages and write out my exploration of them.

6. I write out promises that God makes to me from His Word about specific people or situations.

7. I write out questions that I am asking God. Then, I go back and make notes about what I am coming to understand about them. Some questions I continue to come back to and make notes about for years. For example, years ago I wrote down, *What do you really mean by "dying to myself"?* I have pages of notes that I have added over a period of nearly six years. I am still adding.

These are only a few suggestions for forms journaling can take. Keeping a journal does not have any rules. Find your own ways. You might want to purchase the book *Riches Stored in Secret Places.* It is a devotional guide that introduces the reader to several methods of journaling through Scripture.

Don't feel that you have to journal every single day. Journaling is not to be a burden or another rule to be kept. It is to be a release for you.

Prayer Lists

Be careful how you view prayer lists. Guard against a prayer list prayer life. By that I mean, when you make prayer lists like you make to-do lists for others, it becomes a record of failure. If you list the things you think God should do and then watch to see whether or not He will do them, you will have at least as many unanswered prayers as answered ones. You will develop a misguided theology about prayer. You will misread God's answers.

Instead, use a prayer list to release situations, needs, desires, and people to God. Don't watch to see if He'll answer; watch to see how He answers. Without giving God instructions to follow, list the things that you have committed to Him and the date on which the concern became God's and not yours. Keep a record of His activity in those areas.

How to Use This Journal

I have divided this journal into eight sections with thought starters in each section. This will give you guidance in contemplating and applying God's Word to your daily situations. The thought starters are just tools. Find your own ways to journal.

IN HIS PRESENCE

"You will fill me with joy in your presence, with eternal pleasures at your right hand" (Psalm 16:11 NIV).

End your anxious search, Beloved. To find My presence, look no further than your own heart. I have erected My tabernacle, My dwelling place, in your spirit. You are always in My presence. My presence is My gift to you. Learn to realize and enjoy My presence. I AM everything you need, and I AM in you.

Read:
Acts 17:24
1 Corinthians 3:16
John 14:23

Contemplate the nearness of the Father.

*L*ittle One, the
longing you
feel to know Me
intimately, to live
in My presence, is
but the shadow
cast by My longing
for your presence.
How intensely I
yearn over you.
Relax and let Me
draw you into My
strong arms.

✠

"It is important now that you cease from self-action and self-exerting in attempting to experience His presence. God Himself can act alone."

Experiencing God Through Prayer, Madame Guyon

I am drawing you to Myself— away from the noise and bustle of the world into the wilderness where I can speak tenderly to you. "'Therefore I am now going to allure her; I will lead her into the desert and speak tenderly to her'" (Hos. 2:14 NIV). Go with Me there. Listen for My whisper. I want to give you fresh manna.

✤

"Jesus has pulled you into His inner circle, those to whom He will impart His secrets. Listen. 'I have called you friends, for everything that I learned from my Father I have made known to you' (John 15:15). A person who is following a doctrine need not listen. There is nothing new to know. The one who is following Christ must be continually listening. Spoken prayer is your response to what you have heard."

Heart's Cry,
Jennifer Kennedy Dean

Father, as I soak myself in Your presence, saturate me with Yourself. Seep into my spirit pores until I am filled with You. Let me breathe in Your love for me and breathe it out again toward You. You are my treasure and my heart knows no other home.

✢

"We must know
before we can love. In
order to know God,
we must often think
of Him; and when we
come to love Him, we
shall also think of
Him often, for our
heart will be with our
treasure."

*The Practice of the
Presence of God,*
Bro. Lawrence

In Your presence, I am learning how to love You. You are calling me by Your own glory and excellence. At home with You, I find all my desires converging into one single, overriding desire—to know You. And—unimaginable as it is—You love me and desire my presence.

✣

"Comfort Me, awhile, by letting Me know that you would seek Me just to dwell in My Presence, to be near Me, not even for teaching, not for material gain, not even for a message— but for Me. The longing of the human heart to be loved for itself is something caught from the Great Divine Heart."

God Calling,
Two Listeners

Most High God, Creator of Heaven and Earth, I know that while I am resting in You, You are working in me. While I am focused on You in praise and worship and adoration, thinking of nothing but You, You are working in my inmost being. You are creating desires, authoring ideas, wakening passions that will come to the surface of my thoughts as I carry Your presence into my workday. You are filling me up with rivers of Living Water that will pour out of me all day.

"Be silent to God and He will make and mold you to become the instrument of His purposes. An almighty Will will reinforce your weak will. . . . An all-wise Mind will brood over your mind, awakening it, stimulating it, and making it creative. An all-embracing Love will quicken your love into world-sensitivity until 'He will set the world into your heart.'"

Abundant Living,
E. Stanley Jones

My Heart's Desire, empty me of anything that is cluttering my life and keeping You from having free access. Scrub away my sin stains. Sweep away the shards of broken bric-a-brac. Those things that once distracted me from You have revealed themselves, finally, to be fragile and worthless. The floors of my heart are strewn with their wreckage. Clean out Your dwelling place and fill it with Your glory.

✤

"I know that for the right practice of [the presence of God] the heart must be empty of all other things, because God will possess the heart alone; and as He cannot possess it alone without emptying it of all besides, so neither can He act there, and do in it what He pleases, unless it be left vacant to Him."

The Practice of the Presence of God, Bro. Lawrence

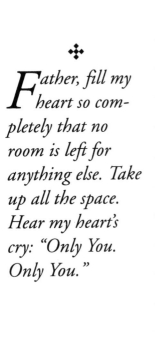

❖

Father, fill my heart so completely that no room is left for anything else. Take up all the space. Hear my heart's cry: "Only You. Only You."

✛

"Our hearts belong to Him alone and He can plant in them His divine desires and make them ours. Enthroned in our lives, He can channel His good plans into the world through our prayers. By allowing our lives to be absorbed in His we can bit by bit be freed of our short-sighted desires and participate in eternity."

The Praying Life,
Jennifer Kennedy Dean

The longer I remain quietly in Your presence, the freer I become. I find that I am no longer weighted down with anxieties. I am no longer bound and restricted by the opinions of others. My feet are no longer immersed in the world's sludge. You have given me feet like the feet of a deer. You enable me to stand on the heights.

✤

Behold, what Love is this
That reaches out for me
And lifts me from the
    miry clay
To set my spirit free

Jennifer Kennedy Dean

Your presence is in me. When I leave my solitude to enter into my world, Your presence goes with me. Teach me to carry the peace and freedom I find in times alone with You into the hustle and bustle of life. Keep me aware of Your presence continually.

❖

"What is here urged
are internal practices
and habits of the
mind. What is here
urged are secret habits
of unceasing orienta-
tion of the deeps of
our being about the
Inward Light, ways of
conducting our
inward life so that we
are perpetually bowed
in worship, while we
are also very busy in
the world of daily
affairs. What is here
urged are inward prac-
tices of the mind at
deepest levels, letting
it swing like the
needle, to the polestar
of the soul."

*A Testament of
Devotion,*
Thomas R. Kelly

Fix Your Eyes on Jesus

"Let us fix our eyes on Jesus, the author and perfecter of our faith" (Heb. 12:2 NIV).

Draw near, My child" is Your sweet call. My heart yearns to enter into Your beckoning Light. The services I have performed for You, the rituals to ensure Your favor, have left me empty. I can't seem to get beyond the veil, where the alluring brightness of Your glory shines.

"Look to My Son. He is the Open Door into My presence. Lose yourself in Him to find your way to Me."

Heart's Cry, Jennifer Kennedy Dean

Read:
John 10:9
John 14:6
Hebrews 10:19–20

Have you been striving to please God? Or have you lost yourself in Jesus?

Jesus, when You moved out of eternity into time; when You left divine order for human chaos; when You traded Your throne for a manger—You had no other reason than love for me. Oh, Lord Jesus, dwell in me in all Your fullness.

It was for me
He took on the time
and space con-
straints of earth
Let a veil of flesh con-
ceal His worth
Set redemption's plan
in motion with His
birth
It was for me.

It was for me
He gave up His
flesh—an offering
for my sin
Let God's wrath
toward me be spent
on Him
Poured out His life so
my life could begin
It was for me.

It was for me
He threw off the time
and space con-
straints of earth
Shed His veil of flesh,
revealed His worth
Opened up for me the
way to Spirit birth
It was for me.

Jennifer Kennedy Dean

Jesus, thank You for being made in the image of man so that I could be remade in the image of You.

❖

"I praise and glorify Thee, O Eternal Wisdom of the Father, for the amazing descent of Thy unattainable Majesty into the common prisonhouse of our mortal nature."

Meditations on the Life of Christ,
Thomas á Kempis

Child of My Heart, for you I gave My Son, My only Son, Whom I love. I took His infinite worth and His majesty and His power and I wrapped them in flesh and laid Him in a manger. Then I laid Him on the altar and there I sacrificed Him— My Son—so that You could know the depths of My love for you. Oh, My child, did you know? The nails that pierced the hands of the Son, pierced the heart of the Father.

✣

"O infinite God, the
brightness of whose
face is often shrouded
from my mortal gaze,
I thank Thee that
Thou didst send Thy
Son Jesus Christ to be
a light in a dark
world. O Christ,
Thou Light of Light, I
thank Thee that in
Thy most holy life
Thou didst pierce the
eternal mystery as
with a great shaft of
heavenly light, so that
in seeing Thee we see
Him whom no man
hath seen at any
time."

*A Diary of Private
Prayer,*
John Baillie

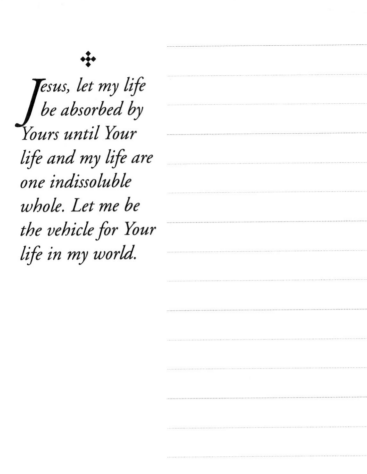

Jesus, let my life be absorbed by Yours until Your life and my life are one indissoluble whole. Let me be the vehicle for Your life in my world.

✛

"On the first day of
Pentecost He
returned, not this time
to be with them exter-
nally—clothed with
that sinless humanity
that God had pre-
pared for Him, being
conceived of the Holy
Spirit in the womb of
Mary—but now to be
in them, imparting to
them His own divine
nature, clothing Him-
self with *their* human-
ity. . . . He spoke with
their lips. He worked
with their hands. This
was the miracle of
new birth, and this
remains the very heart
of the Gospel!"

*The Saving Life of
Christ,*
Major W. Ian Thomas

❖

*Jesus, I am awed
and forever
grateful for the
work You have
done for me. Now
I hunger to know
the fullness of the
work You will do
in me.*

✣

"His Life in me is creating desires that match God's will. 'It is God who works in you to will . . . his good purpose' (Phil. 2:13). He is expressing His desires through my desires so that when I ask whatever I will, I am asking according to His will. He is causing my will to come into alignment with His. To know God's will so that I will know how to pray with power, I must trust His Life operating in me."

Power Praying,
Jennifer Kennedy Dean

My Child, you were created for one purpose— to be the vessel into which I pour My life. Until you are a container for Me, you are not truly yourself. That sense of disconnect- edness and alien- ation, the feeling that you are all alone and unable to fill the void in your center—that's your heart's cry. I have heard the cry of my people.

✤

"When I am in him, I
am in the Kingdom
of God
And in the Fatherland
of my Soul."

Walter Rauschenbusch,
D. R. Sharpe

Jesus, teach me to surrender to the power of Your life in me. Remind me that my efforts to help You only hinder You. Show me how to yield to Your work in me.

✣

"The freer you are from exerting your own effort, the more quickly you will move toward your Lord.

"Why is this? Because there is a divine energy drawing you. When this divine energy is completely unhindered, *He* has complete liberty to draw you just as He pleases.

"Jesus Christ is the great magnet of your soul, but of your soul only. He will not draw the impurities and mixtures that are mingled with it. Any such impurities prevent His full power of attraction. . . .

"Observe the ocean. The water in the ocean begins to evaporate. Then the vapor begins moving toward the sun. As the vapor leaves the earth, it is full of impurities; however, as it ascends, it becomes more refined and more purified.

"What did the vapor do? The vapor did nothing. . . . The purifying took place as the vapor was drawn up into the heavens!"

Experiencing the Depths of Jesus Christ,
Jeanne Guyon

Christ in me, shaping me in His image—my hope of glory! The only hope I have of fulfilling my destiny—to be the outshining of His brightness. Christ, my life.

✥

"If you are to know the fulness of life in Christ, you are to appropriate the efficacy of *what He is.* . . . Relate everything, moment by moment as it arises, to the adequacy *of what He is in you,* and assume that His adequacy will be operative. . . . Simply expose by faith every situation as it arises, to the all-sufficiency of the One who indwells you by His life. Can any situation possibly arise, in any circumstances, for which He is not adequate? Any pressure, promise, problem, responsibility or temptation for which the Lord Jesus Himself is not adequate? If He be truly God, there cannot be a single one!"

The Saving Life of Christ,
Major W. Ian Thomas

*Jesus, in You I
find all that the
Father offers. You
are the storehouse
of His riches. You
are the coffer that
holds His treasures.
Everything He dis-
penses, He routes
through You. All
that belongs to the
Father belongs to
You. It is Yours to
give. Apart from
You, the riches of
the Father cannot
reach me. You are
all I need. Having
You, I have all.*

✠

"To pray is nothing
more involved than to
let Jesus into our
needs. To pray is to
give Jesus permission
to employ His powers
in the alleviation of
our distress. To pray is
to let Jesus glorify His
name in the midst of
our needs. . . . To pray
is nothing more
involved than to open
the door, giving Jesus
access to our needs
and permitting Him
to exercise His own
power in dealing with
them."

Prayer,
O. Hallesby

KEEP IN STEP WITH THE SPIRIT

"Since we live by the Spirit, let us keep in step with the Spirit" (Gal. 5:25 NIV).

Spirit of the Living God, You are the heat that fuses me into the body and makes me one with my brothers and sisters in Christ. As I yield to Your work, keeping in step with You, I find myself more and more living in peace with those around me.

"While there are many different kinds of fellowship, there is spiritual fellowship which is much more than the exchange of ideas and opinions. It is the interaction of spirits. This kind of fellowship is possible only after our outward man is shattered and our spirit is thus released to touch the spirit of others. In this sharing of spirit we experience the fellowship of the saints and understand what the Scriptures mean by 'fellowship in the Spirit.' It truly is a fellowship in the Spirit, and not an interflow of ideas. By this fellowship in the Spirit we can pray with one accord."

The Release of the Spirit, Watchman Nee

Read:
John 17:20–23,26
Ephesians 4:2–6

Do you hear Jesus' deep desire for His own to be united through
His Spirit? Do you embrace the extension of that desire—that all of
His children would be one through His Spirit?

*The Spirit's
quiet whisper
Bids me bow
before Your throne
Till my heart's
deepest yearnings
Are the echo of
Your own.*

*Jennifer Kennedy
Dean*

"The whole secret of prayer is found in these three words, *in the Spirit*. God the Father answers the prayer that God the Holy Spirit inspires. ... True prayer is prayer in the Spirit; that is the prayer the Spirit inspires and directs. ... The Spirit knows the will of God. If I pray in the Spirit and look to the Spirit to teach me God's will, He will lead me out in prayer along the line of that will. He will give me faith that the prayer is to be answered."

How to Pray,
R. A. Torrey

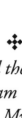

*God the Spirit,
I am Your
temple. My pur-
pose for being on
the earth is to con-
tain You. Until
You fill me com-
pletely, I am not
functioning at my
capacity. Dwell in
me richly.*

✣

"Remember again that the creature has no other end to his existence than to be a manifestor of the Creator—God in man, and God through man; and that therefore a human being is not true human until he is a temple of the Holy Spirit. Nothing can function except by the laws of its being; a car won't go unless its machinery works aright; and a man can never be a man unless he is a God-indwelt, God-controlled man, because men are not made to 'work' any other way."

The Deep Things of God,
Norman P. Grubb

Spirit of Prayer, before a desire has even become a conscious thought—before I have defined it and assigned words to it—You have prayed it through me. While it was no more than an inarticulate inner groaning, You expressed it to the Father. By the time I can speak it, the answer is already prepared. Before I called, He heard and while I was yet speaking, He answered.

"Before a word is on my tongue, you know it completely, O Lord" (Psalm 139:4 NIV).

"There come times when prayer pours forth in volumes and originality such as we cannot create. It rolls through us like a mighty tide. Our prayers are mingled with a vaster Word, a Word that at one time was made flesh. We pray, and yet it is not we who pray, but a Greater who prays in us. . . . All we can say is, Prayer is taking place, and I am given to be in the orbit."

A Testament of Devotion,
Thomas R. Kelly

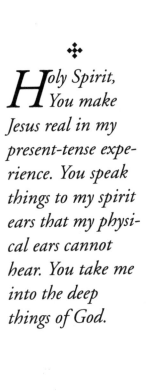

*H*oly Spirit, You make Jesus real in my present-tense experience. You speak things to my spirit ears that my physical ears cannot hear. You take me into the deep things of God.

✛

They tell me, Lord, that
    when I seem
    To be in speech with
    you,
Since but one voice is
    heard, it's all a dream,
    One talker aping two.

Sometimes it is, yet not as
    they
    Conceive it. Rather, I
Seek in myself the things I
    hoped to say,
    But lo!, my wells are dry.

Then, seeing me empty,
    you forsake
    The listener's role and
    through
My dumb lips breathe and
    into utterance wake
    The thoughts I never
    knew.

And thus you neither need
    reply
    Nor can; thus, while we
    seem
Two talkers, thou art One
    forever, and I
    No dreamer, but thy
    dream.

Letters to Malcolm,
C. S. Lewis

❖

*Spirit of Truth,
fill me so com-
pletely that no
room is left for pre-
tense. Stand guard
over my heart—
never let me hide
behind religious
words and rituals
to mask a cold and
empty center.*

✣

"The danger of religious formalities is that they may replace spiritual worship. This happened to the religious leaders of Jesus' day. They knew every detail of the ceremonial forms of worship, but when the intended object of their worship stood before them, they did not recognize Him. They had become so intent on the methods that they missed the truth. . . . Outward forms of worship were intended to express true, inward worship. The danger is that they will disguise inward emptiness. The Holy Spirit is the guard against empty, surface religion."

Heart's Cry,
Jennifer Kennedy Dean

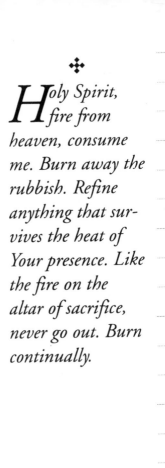

✥

Holy Spirit, fire from heaven, consume me. Burn away the rubbish. Refine anything that survives the heat of Your presence. Like the fire on the altar of sacrifice, never go out. Burn continually.

"On God's anvil. Perhaps you've been there.

"Melted down. Formless. Undone. . . .
   "An instrument is useful only if it's in the right shape. A dull ax or a bent screwdriver needs attention, and so do we. A good blacksmith keeps his tools in shape. So does God.
   "Should God place you on his anvil, be thankful. It means he thinks you're still worth reshaping."

On the Anvil,
Max Lucado

Spirit, You are the promised power from on high. If You indwell me, then all the power of God indwells me. Teach me to get out of Your way, to stop hindering the flow of Your power. Draw my gaze away from my inability to focus on Your ability. You are able.

❖

I am a mighty power
within you.
The only time you are
weak, My child,
is when you choose to
live
in your own strength,
not Mine.
I give you the power
to live in radiant
intensity of joy
and power and enthu-
siasm
at the highest level of
My Spirit's ability.
From this moment on
refer to weakness not
as an enemy,
for weakness opens
the way to My
power.

*His Thoughts Toward
Me,*
Marie Chapian

Spirit Breath, my physical nature draws its life-sustaining resources from the earth. I breathe the earth's air. I eat the earth's food. I wear the earth's clothes. Earth is the proper environment for my physical nature. But my spirit nature must draw its life-sustaining resources from heaven. I must breathe in Spirit; I must eat Spirit food; I must clothe myself in Christ. You are the point of contact between my spirit nature housed on earth and my resources in heaven. You are my lifeline, my connection.

✢

"Prayer is . . . the opening of a channel from your emptiness to God's fullness."

Abundant Living,
E. Stanley Jones

❖

*Spirit of God,
show me the
reality of the invis-
ible world—the
world of Spirit.*

✛

"Forbid, O Lord God, that my thoughts today should be wholly occupied with the world's passing show. Seeing that in Thy lovingkindness Thou hast given me the power to lift my mind to the contemplation of things unseen and eternal, forbid that I should remain content with the things of sense and time. Grant rather that each day may do something to strengthen my hold upon the unseen world, so to increase my sense of its reality, and so to attach my heart to its holy interests that, as the end of my earthly life draws ever nearer, I may not grow to be a part of these fleeting earthly surroundings, but rather grow more and more conformed to the life of the world to come."

A Diary of Private Prayer,
John Baillie

❖

BE FILLED WITH THE KNOWLEDGE OF HIS WILL

"We have not stopped praying for you and asking God to fill you with the knowledge of his will through all spiritual wisdom and understanding" (Col. 1:9 NIV).

My Child, you are highly favored in heaven. You are privy to My secrets. I have decreed that you have the authority to access all of My riches. The forces of heaven are on alert, ready to spring into action at your call. I want to show you what belongs to you so that you will know what to ask for.

"Sometimes we mistake His 'will' for His 'ways.' . . . I'm learning not to confuse what He's doing with how He's doing it."

Power Praying, Jennifer Kennedy Dean

Read:
1 Corinthians 2:12
John 15:15
John 16:12–15

Do you believe that the Father wants you to know His will? Do you want to know the Father's will?

Quester, I see your search. I know that you are conscientiously seeking My will. You want to live and pray with power. Relax. When you are resting in Me, My will finds you.

❖

"Even the most ordinary idea, thought, or activity is often Him moving us to do His will. When we act on what seems to be a random choice, we often find ourselves right in the middle of 'the good works, which God prepared in advance for us to do' (Eph. 2:10). . . . We walk continually in the flow of His will as He releases His power from our spirit center into our personalities, intellects, will, emotions, and desires. He reproduces His will in us. We begin to understand faith as rest, rather than faith as work. While our bodies are busy carrying out His will, our minds and emotions are resting in Him."

Riches Stored in Secret Places,
Jennifer Kennedy Dean

*Darling Child,
you want Me
to give you a
detailed course of
action. You think
that if you could
only know how
and when, then
you could have
faith. But I will
never do that
because I am grow-
ing your capacity
to trust Me. I am
teaching you how
to rely on your
spiritual senses. I
will show you the
direction I am
going, but not how
I'll get there. Learn
the adventure of
watching My will
unfold.*

✛

"He, the God of the Universe, confined Himself within the narrow limits of a Baby-form and . . . submitted to your human limitations, and you have to learn that your vision and power, boundless as far as spiritual things are concerned, must in temporal affairs submit to limitations too."

God Calling,
Two Listeners

Spirit Child, I am clearly revealing My will to your spiritual senses. Learn to use them and learn to trust them. They are in your spiritual genetic code; You inherited them from Me.

✥

"When you were born into the physical world you were born with a set of physical senses. These are the senses by which you interpret, understand, and interact with your physical world. . . . You have learned that your physical senses are reliable. . . . When you were born into the kingdom of God, you were born with a set of spiritual senses. . . . Your spiritual senses are the means by which you know, understand, and respond to your spiritual world. . . . Faith is your God-given capacity to receive and act on spiritual knowledge. . . . You can be sure about the knowledge you receive by means of your spiritual senses."

The Praying Life,
Jennifer Kennedy Dean

*F*aith Seeker, I know that you feel insecure about your spiritual senses. I know that to you they seem less real, less substantial and reliable, than your physical senses. But that is only because you have not practiced using them enough. I will only require of you that which your spiritual senses are mature enough to perceive. They will mature and sharpen with use.

✛

"Your faith will increase as your spiritual senses mature. When a baby is born into the physical world, that baby has the sense of sight, but cannot distinguish and identify shapes. The baby has the sense of hearing, but cannot divide sounds into words and ascribe meaning to them. The baby's senses have to mature over time and with practice. It is the same with your spiritual senses. Knowing how to hear God clearly and reliably is learned by the slow discipline of prayer and obedience. God will guide you steadily and gently."

The Praying Life,
Jennifer Kennedy Dean

*My Beloved,
You choose
how much of My
will you really
want to know. You
will know as much
of My will as you
are ready to put
into practice.
You've already
heard Me, but
you've closed your
ears. When you act
on what you know
right now, I will
take you deeper.
Today, when you
hear My voice, do
not harden your
heart.*

✤

"And the longer and more beautiful the Lion sang, the harder Uncle Andrew tried to make himself believe that he could hear nothing but roaring. Now the trouble about trying to make yourself stupider than you really are is that you very often succeed. Uncle Andrew did. He soon did hear nothing but roaring in Aslan's song. Soon he couldn't have heard anything else even if he had wanted to."

The Magician's
Nephew,
C. S. Lewis

✤

*L*istener, if you want to hear Me, you have to trust My ability to speak to you.

✢

"We find in [George Muller's] journal frequent mention made of his spending two or three hours in prayer over the word for the feeding of his spiritual life. As the fruit of this, when he had need of strength and encouragement in prayer, the individual promises were not to him so many arguments from a book to be used with God, but living words which he had heard the Father's living voice speak to him, and which he could now bring to the Father in living faith."

With Christ in the School of Prayer, Andrew Murray

Child, you will find My will written in My Word, but only when the Living Word, My Son, is speaking it to you. Listen for My voice in My Word. Don't look for cut-and-dried, prepackaged formulas when I have fresh truth for you. Today, hear My voice.

✣

"Prayer is an integral part of the cosmos. It is the spiritual 'token of exchange,' whereby the commodities of the unseen are brought into the possession of Man, who lives both in the unseen and the seen. . . . The thought is tremendous. My friend, when you and I feel drawn to Prayer, it is God desirous of pouring forth His heart: the great depths of the thoughts of God—of His desires—seeking to find expression through such imperfect channels as you and me."

The Dynamic of All-Prayer,
G. Granger Fleming

Child, when you don't know My will, you do know My heart. You can be confident that My will in any situation is good, acceptable, and perfect. You do not have to be able to put My will into words in order to pray My will. My Son is teaching you the most powerful and effective prayer of all: "Let Your kingdom come; let Your will be done." You point to the need; I will apply My power.

✢

"This power is so rich
and so mobile that all
we have to do when
we pray is to point to
the persons or things
to which we desire to
have this power
applied, and He, the
Lord of this power,
will direct the neces-
sary power to the
desired place at once."

Prayer,
O. Hallesby

Little One, you can always know this about My will: it is My will to meet your need and fulfill your desire. One way that I show you what I want to do is by allowing needs and desires into your life. By allowing them in, I am announcing to you My willing-ness—My eager-ness—to apply My power in your life.

✛

"What are the circumstances in your life that look overwhelming and impossible? Now place them against the backdrop of the amazing power and astonishing love of God. Do they look different now? Do you see them as they are? Every circumstance, every need, every desire is God's entry point into your life. Every difficulty is simply highlighting the exact place where God will apply His power. Every challenge or obstacle is God's opportunity to substantiate His promises. Problems are nothing more than labor pains as God brings about the birth of His vision."

Power Praying,
Jennifer Kennedy Dean

BUILD UP ONE ANOTHER

"Encourage one another and build each other up"
(1 Thess. 5:11 NIV).

My Children, though you may not feel it, you are all one. You cannot tear down another without diminishing yourself. When you build up another, you increase your own strength. Through you, My Spirit children born of My incorruptible seed and filled with My eternal life, I display My fullness.

Read:
Ephesians 1:22–23
Ephesians 2:14–18

Let the Father impress upon you His heart's cry for unity among
His children.

*L*ittle Flock,
where among
you is bitterness
flourishing? Each
of you, examine
your own relation-
ships within the
body. As far as it is
up to you, are you
keeping peace? Are
you protecting
unity? Are your
words promoting
instruction? Or are
they separating
brothers? My pur-
pose is to unite;
Satan's purpose is
to divide. Whose
purpose are you
establishing?

✢

"God's desire is to provide safety, protection, and blessing in a company of believers. Satan's demons work overtime to provoke sins of slander, backbiting, gossip, hatred, and a host of other destructive attitudes and actions designed to destroy the body of Christ. As a result, God's people are isolated from each other and are left vulnerable to more insidious attacks by the enemy. And the enemy takes full advantage of these moments of discord in our relationships to generate resentments and bitternesses that separate and destroy."

Create in Me a Clean Heart,
Ray Beeson

Sheep of My Pasture, My examining is making you uncomfortable. You want to justify yourself to Me— to tell Me how wronged you've been. Underlying all your sin crust is a core of fear that if you forgive your brother or sister completely, cancel out the debt owed, the wrong done to you may never be avenged and properly punished. You resent My mercy when it is directed toward someone who owes you an apology; and you are refusing to be the channel of My misdirected grace.

✣

INDISCRETION

I do not hate You,
  God.
Please understand.
You are OK, A-One,
the Very Best,
second to none I
  know,
great and beyond
my criticism so
I say Amen
to You and all Your
  good
intentions—but
I might be right about
Your indiscretion in
forgiving folks
gladly and shamelessly
upon the least
evidence of regret.
I think
You carry love too far.

You! Jonah!
Thomas John Carlisle

*O*ffspring of
My Spirit,
bitterness is not at
home in you. I
indwell you, and
your life is not the
natural environ-
ment for bitterness
to root and grow.
It is a weed, a fruit
destroyer, an
invader. It is sap-
ping your joy and
stunting your
growth. Let Me
have it and I will
uproot it. Unable
to receive nourish-
ment, it will
wither and die.
You will be free.
Give Me your
permission to
begin the process.

❖

"Weed out bitterness. Let praise take root and flourish. Cultivate my life so that it will display Your beauty. Make my life like a watered garden, lush with the Spirit's fruit."

Heart's Cry,
Jennifer Kennedy Dean

My Well-watered Garden, I am beginning My uprooting project by digging underneath the root. Let Me show you what I found there. Give attention to Me while I shovel out the muck that nourished the root of bitterness. What made the offense offensive? What unhealed wound did it touch? What unsurrendered pride did it awaken? What insecurity did it unmask? What uncrucified flesh did it discover?

❖

Sin
Crouching at my door
Deviously
Watching for the
    opportune moment
To pounce.

Sin
Probing for uncrucified
    life
Flesh with vital signs
To massage into
    viability
And master.

Jennifer Kennedy Dean

*Crucified Ones,
now—deal the
final death blow to
stubborn flesh that
refuses to die. Don't
hesitate because your
emotions are not
aligned with My pur-
pose. Only I can
change your heart, so
don't try to do My job.
Pray for the one who
wronged you. Pray
blessings and abun-
dance for the one you
are in the process of
forgiving. Pour your
anger and hurt out to
Me, but pour My
mercy out to your
brother. I promise to
give you opportunities
to lift up and promote
your offender. Do it,
keep on doing it, and
soon you will be as
you should be—all
glorious within.*

✥

CAPTURED
Ensnared in our
    revenge
we die until
we claim the privilege
of sharing His
unerring mercy.

You! Jonah!
Thomas John Carlisle

Bride, as a bridegroom rejoices over his bride, so I rejoice over you. A faithful wife—a wife of noble character—you are My treasure and the source of My joy. I will display you as My signet ring. Because of you, all will perceive and recognize My power and authority. You, bride, speak with wisdom; faithful instruction is on your tongue. Your words now are the overflow of your pure and poison-free heart.

✤

"He is cheered and He beams with exceeding joy and takes pleasure in your presence. He has engraved a place for Himself in you and there He quietly rests in His love and affection for you. He cannot contain Himself at the thought of you and with the greatest joy spins around wildly in anticipation over you . . . and has placed you above all other creations and in the highest place in His priorities. In fact, he shouts and sings in triumph joyfully proclaiming the gladness of His heart in a song of rejoicing! All because of you!"

Translation of Zephaniah 3:17 by Dennis Jernigan

My Body, when you see how ingeniously I have put you together, you will understand that the jealousy, turf guarding, and competition that define the world's interactions are a cell-destroying cancer when they invade My body. I have placed each of you into the body as a cell with a specific function that only you can fill. When you receive an instruction from the head, each of you responds to it according to your cell function. Your diverse reactions and differing responses are the coordinated action of the body at work.

❖

"The final grounds of holy Fellowship are in God. Lives immersed and drowned in God are drowned in love, and know one another in Him, and know one another in love. . . . Such lives have a common meeting-point; they live in a common joyous enslavement. They go back into a single Center where they are at home with Him and with one another. It is as if every soul had a final base, and that final base of every soul is one single Holy Ground, shared in by all. . . . He is actively moving in all, co-ordinating those who are pliant to His will and suffusing them all with His glory and His joy."

A Testament of Devotion,
Thomas R. Kelly

My Heirs, each of you, pass along the riches I invest in you. You are not to be reservoirs, but channels. I have placed the gifts of My Spirit among you. Gifts—not possessions. Things given are gifts; things hoarded are possessions. It is the act of giving away that transforms the thing.

✤

"I am revealing so much to you. Pass it on. Each truth is a jewel. Some poor spirit-impoverished friend will be glad of it. Drop one here and there.

"Seek to find a heart-home for each Truth I have imparted to you. More Truths will flow in. Use all I give you. Help others. I ache to find a way into each life and heart, for all to cry expectantly, 'Even so, come Lord Jesus.'"

God Calling,
Two Listeners

My Army, I have given you the one essential element necessary for taking possession of all My promises: prayer. Prayer is the muscle structure that wields the weapons of your warfare and makes them operative. I have placed this secret weapon in your hands so that you can destroy the strongholds of the enemy and set captives free. The whole spiritual world is on notice. When you, My church, announce with one voice My manifold wisdom, the spiritual realm must deploy accordingly.

✤

"All walls shall fall before you, too. There is no earth-power. It falls like a house of paper, at My miracle-working touch. Your faith and My power— the only two essentials. Nothing else is needed.

"So, if man's petty opposition still holds good it is only because I choose to let it stand between you and what would be a mistake for you. If not—a word— a thought—from Me, and it is gone. The hearts of Kings are in My rule and government. All men can be moved at My wish."

God Calling,
Two Listeners

❖

SEEK THE KINGDOM

"But seek first his kingdom and his righteousness, and all these things will be given to you as well" (Matt. 6:33 NIV).

Citizen of My Kingdom, I have already transferred your citizenship from the world kingdom to My kingdom. The world kingdom is limited to the boundaries of time and space and senses; My kingdom has no limits—no boundaries imposed by geography, no restraints dictated by time, no finite apprehension of truth narrowly defined by sense knowledge. You are now a citizen and inhabitant of the kingdom of power and eternity. The riches of My kingdom are at your disposal. Seek the kingdom—study the landscape, learn the governing principles, become acquainted with the natural resources—so that you can make full use of your citizenship.

Read:
Luke 12:32
Colossians 1:13
Ephesians 1:3
Ephesians 2:6

Set your heart to seek the kingdom.

Heir to My Riches, understand this kingdom principle: Because you are fully enstated as a citizen of My kingdom, you never have to worry about anything. All the energy that citizens of the world kingdom expend scurrying after earth supplies, you will put to eternal use. Everything you need to operate in the earth environment, I have already set aside and earmarked for you. It is yours. Turn your energy and your passion to seeking and possessing kingdom riches.

108

✤

"A settled peace . . . is
the most frequent
experience of those
who have trod the
path of relinquish-
ment. . . . Frequently
we hold on so tightly
to the good that we do
know that we cannot
receive the greater
good that we do not
know. God has to help
us let go of our tiny
vision in order to
release the greater
good he has in store
for us."

Prayer,
Richard J. Foster

✤

Joint heir with My Son, I have given you the legal designation of joint heir with Jesus. Do you know what that entails? It means that you and Jesus are copossessors of My kingdom. Joint heirs do not split the inheritance between them; they jointly own everything. Whatever I have given to Jesus belongs to you! Think about it—I loved you so much that I did not withhold My only and deeply beloved Son. I have given you the very core of My heart—the One most precious to Me and most valued by Me. Would I, then, withhold anything from you? Have no anxiety about anything.

✢

"I meet today, today. I
do not telescope all
next week into today.
I clip off all my
engagements one by
one as a person clips
off coupons. . . . I do
not take any worries
to bed with me.
Bishop Quayle tells of
lying awake, trying to
hold the world
together by his worry-
ing, when God said,
'Now, William, you
go to sleep and I'll sit
up.'"

Abundant Living,
E. Stanley Jones

*Child, I know all
about the situation
that is worrying you right
now. I knew about it
before you did. Believe Me
when I tell you it is finished. Your prayers are
bringing the finished work
out of the spiritual realm
to establish it in the material realm. You do not see
the finished work in the
earth environment yet, but
earth is not your home. Do
you know why you are
having difficulty believing
right now? Because you
have only looked at the situation in the artificial
light of the earth kingdom.
Earth kingdom's light only
shows up the need. Bring
it to Me. Spend time with
Me in your true kingdom.
Look at it in the Eternal
Light. I will blot out the
need and illumine only the
supply. Come!*

✣

"The real difficulty is
. . . to adapt ones
steady beliefs about
tribulation to this par-
ticular tribulation: for
the particular, when it
arrives, always *seems* so
peculiarly intolerable."

Letters of C. S. Lewis,
C. S. Lewis

Beloved, I am watching over you continually. My eye never wanders. I never fall asleep. You are always, always in My care. You do not have to perform rituals that will attract My attention. You have My full attention every minute of every day. You cannot ask more of Me than I am longing to give. Ask! Ask! And keep on asking!

"When I was too busy with my petty concerns to remember Thee, Thou with a universe to govern wert not too busy to remember me."

A Diary of Private Prayer,
John Baillie

"None ever sought Me in vain. I wait, wait with a hungry longing to be called upon; and I, who have already seen your hearts' needs before you cried upon Me, before perhaps you were conscious of those needs yourself, I am already preparing the answer."

God Calling,
Two Listeners

Darling One, you must remember that what takes you by surprise does not take Me by surprise. Anything that touches you has been scrutinized and carefully evaluated by Me. You are one of My honored and cherished kingdom dwellers. You are under My protection. It only reaches you if I have determined that the pain it causes will be outweighed by the glory it brings. I have not let it touch you until I have pre-pared you, prepared every circumstance, put every piece in place. The situation that is causing you pain and anxiety right now is not a punishment; it is not because you have not found the correct prayer method. Cooperate with Me and you will find the eternal weight of glory secreted away in your situation.

✣

"That is the secret!
You co-operate with
the immediate
inevitable because you
know that in and
through things God's
will is being worked
out, and that Will
wills your good."

Abundant Living,
E. Stanley Jones

My Friend, as you learn more how to live in My kingdom while existing on the earth, you are noticing changes—some so subtle that they've been in place for some time before you recognize them. Do you know why? It's because your earthbound will, the will that your flesh birthed, cannot thrive in the environment of My kingdom. My kingdom is not its natural habitat. As the natural course of things, your little will is dying and being replaced by My perfect will.

✤

"Little by little we are changed by this daily crucifixion of the will. Changed, not like a tornado changes things, but like a grain of sand in an oyster changes things. . . . Please remember, we are dealing with the crucifixion of the will, not the obliteration of the will. Crucifixion always has resurrection tied to it. God is not destroying the will but transforming it so that over a process of time and experience we can freely will what God wills."

Prayer,
Richard J. Foster

My Child, the defining attribute of My kingdom is joy. This is not a solemn place. Here, in My house, is a banquet, a forever celebration—dancing and singing and laughter. As you are making the transition from one kingdom to the other, as your eyes are adjusting to a new light, you may not have realized the joy yet. But come on! Just ahead of you, just a few more steps, you are almost to the banquet hall.

❖

Leaving old
Embracing New
Escaping boundaries
Embracing Infinity
Fleeing darkness
Embracing Light
Forsaking emptiness
Embracing Joy

Jennifer Kennedy Dean

*Light Bearer, when
you were born
into My kingdom, My
kingdom was born
into you. My kingdom
is flowing out of you
onto the earth. Little
you—you are the
leaven that will
leaven the whole loaf;
you are the mustard
seed that will grow to
a tree-sized plant.
Don't look at your lit-
tleness, look at My
greatness. Every act of
faith and obedience
puts My kingdom into
the earth environ-
ment. Every time you
speak My name, every
time you act My love,
every time you tell My
truth—kingdom light
overcomes earth dark-
ness. In that place at
that time, My king-
dom comes.*

✤

"The true prophetic message always calls us to a spiritual defiance of the world as it is now. Our prayer, to the extent that it is fully authentic, undermines the status quo. It is a spiritual underground resistance movement."

Prayer,
Richard J. Foster

*Kingdom Child,
before you were
born into My king-
dom, while I was
waiting for your
arrival, I prepared
for you. I laid the
table and prepared
the fatted calf. I
made you a robe and
fitted a ring for your
finger. I anticipated
your entrance with
such joy. I could
hardly wait until you
got here. I kept whis-
pering to you—
telling you what I
had prepared for you
in the kingdom of
My light. When I
saw you coming, I
was so excited that I
ran to meet you and
led you home. It gives
Me deep pleasure to
see you use and enjoy
your inheritance.*

✥

"Try and see a Mother
preparing birthday or
Christmas delights for
her child—the while
her Mother-heart
sings: 'Will she not
love that? How she
will love this!' and
anticipates the rapture
of her child, her own
heart full of the ten-
derest joy. Where did
the Mother learn all
this preparation—joy?
From Me—a faint
echo this of My prepa-
ration—joy. Try to see
this as plans unfold of
My preparing."

God Calling,
Two Listeners

CHANGED INTO HIS IMAGE

"We, who with unveiled faces all reflect the Lord's glory, are being transformed into his likeness with ever-increasing glory, which comes from the Lord, who is the Spirit" (2 Cor. 3:18 NIV).

I embrace my destiny—to become the Son's reflection, just as the Son is the Father's reflection. I say yes to the transforming power of His life in me. I yield to His work as He moves me from one degree of glory to the next.

Read:
Romans 8:29
John 15:5
Colossians 1:25–27

Will you lay aside everything you have counted on to give you value, or glory? Will you abandon every hope but One? Christ in you.

My Sculpture, I am sculpting you into a perfect expression of Myself in the world. You are My work of art. I take such time and care with you—chiseling, sanding, shaping. When you are finished, you will be a masterpiece, worthy of bearing My name. When you resist My work, you distort My expression.

✛

"Every sin is the distortion of an energy breathed into us. . . . We poison the wine as He decants it into us; murder a melody he would play with us as the instrument. We caricature the self-portrait He would paint. Hence all sin, whatever else it is, is sacrilege."

Letters to Malcolm, C. S. Lewis

My Self-portrait, your inner life is the canvas on which I am painting. I am painting you against the background of eternity. It brings out your best features. Day by day, brush stroke by brush stroke, I am perfecting My work. When I am finished, it will be like looking in a mirror.

✜

"What is the process by which we come to reflect Him? 'And we who with unveiled faces all reflect the Lord's glory, are being changed into his likeness with ever-increasing glory, which comes from the Lord, who is the Spirit' (2 Cor. 3:18). . . . Paul is telling us that because we are in the Lord's presence, we [like Moses] reflect His glory as a mirror reflects an image. . . . How does a mirror reflect? It absorbs light bouncing off an object and projects it back in exactly the same configuration. It absorbs and reflects. As we absorb Him . . . we are being changed into an exact reflection of Him. We are being transformed— changed from the inside out; structurally changed. . . . How is this changing being accomplished? 'Which comes from the Lord, who is the Spirit.' The Spirit is doing the changing as we continue in His presence."

Power Praying,
Jennifer Kennedy Dean

131

My Image, it is My job to transform you; it is your job to be accessible. At first, you will need to discipline yourself and consciously remember to keep your life open to Me. Later, with practice, it will become your holy habit. It will not always be work— soon it will be rest. Put in the continual will-surrendering work so that you can make it to the more mature level—rest. Strive to enter My rest.

✣

"But longer discipline in this inward prayer will establish more enduring upreachings of praise and submission and relaxed listening in the depths, unworded but habitual orientation of all one's self about Him who is the Focus. The process is much simpler now. Little glances, quiet breathings of submission and invitation suffice. . . . Behind the foreground of the words continues the background of heavenly orientation, as all the currents of our being set toward Him. Through the shimmering light of divine presence we look out upon the world, and in its turmoil and fitfulness, we may be given to respond, in some increased measure, in ways dimly suggestive of the Son of Man."

A Testament of Devotion,
Thomas R. Kelly

Clay in My Hands, I need soft clay. Each act of disobedience hardens your heart toward Me. Sin by sin, if unconfessed, you grow more brittle and less moldable. Each time you refuse My voice, My voice becomes harder for you to hear. But each act of obedience softens you. Obedience by obedience, you become softer in My hands, easier to mold. I can make you into something altogether new.

✤

"There is such a thing as coming into such sweet relation to the will of God that we are fused into oneness with it. HIS WILL BECOMES OURS, and He gladly sets us free to carry out our own wishes—they really being His first and then ours."

The Dynamic of All-Prayer,
G. Granger Fleming

Heart Reflection, don't feel discouraged because you seem to be meeting the same sin pattern in yourself over and over again. You think I must be becoming impatient—that I must be disappointed in you because you have to confess the same sin over and over again. I don't grow weary. I'm not disappointed. You see, I knew all along it was there. I want you to recognize its hold and long for freedom from it. I won't let you bury it or disguise it anymore. This experience is a cleansing process. Part of My cleansing process is a desert walk: you have to be convinced of your own inability. The second part is living in the Promised Land: you finally turn away from your own efforts and look to My power. I am able to perfect what concerns you.

❖

A heart like Yours,
my one desire.
Do Your work,
Refiner's Fire.

Jennifer Kennedy Dean

*M*y Tabernacle,
as you yield
to Me, I am refo-
cusing your pas-
sions and refining
your vision. You
look more like Me
every day.

✣

"Just as the moon cannot be reflected well on a restless sea, so God cannot get to an unquiet mind. 'Be still, and know'; be unstill and you do not know— God cannot get to you. In the stillness the prayer itself may be corrected. For God does not only answer prayer; He also corrects prayer and makes it more answerable. One night I bowed my head in silent prayer before a sermon and whispered to God, 'O God, help me.' Very quickly came back the reply: 'I will do something better; I will use you.'

"That amendment was decidedly better. I was asking God to help me—I was the center; I was calling to God for my own purposes. But 'I will use you' meant I was not the center; something beyond me was the center and I was only the instrument of that purpose beyond myself. God's answer shifted the whole center of gravity of the prayer."

Abundant Living,
E. Stanley Jones

*W*ork of My Hands, I know that sometimes My sculpting hurts. Sometimes you feel as though you are looking less like Me rather than more like Me. Don't worry. It's just a stage in the sculpting process. There are intervals in the work of precisely shaping you during which you look like a shapeless, formless lump of clay. Your old shape has been destroyed, but your new shape has not yet emerged. Don't give up. I am the Master Artist. Those are My hands you feel squeezing you and pushing you. I know exactly what I'm doing.

140

✤

Infinite Patience
Meticulous attention
  to detail
Consuming focus
Perfectionist

Master Potter
Lovingly shaping
Vessels of His Mercy

Jennifer Kennedy Dean

Vessel of My Life, don't be discouraged because it seems I am not answering your prayers. You are allowing your disappointment to give you a spiritual inferiority complex. You are beginning to doubt that I care at all. "Maybe they're right after all," you say. "Maybe God is too big to get involved in my little affairs. Maybe He is too busy for me." No, child, every step you take and every thought you think are infinitely precious to Me. Right now is a season for learning to move deeper into the kingdom. I am teaching you the difference between the desires of the moment and the desires of your heart.

"Rows of beautiful trees were laid low in a storm. Reason? The water was too near the surface; so the trees did not have to put their roots deep down to find water; hence the tragedy. God may deny us a surface answer in order to get us to put our roots deeper into eternal reality, so that in some future storm we shall be unmoved."

Abundant Living,
E. Stanley Jones

Blessed One, part of the shaping is done by fire. But it is not a destroying fire; it is a cleansing fire. When you walk through it, it will not burn you. It will refine you. I am in the fire. It is going to burn away the earth stuff still clinging to you. It is going to set the work I have finished so that the shape is stable. Once you've walked through the fire and have seen for yourself that you are invulnerable to any power except Mine, you will be My fearless warrior.

❖

"'Hero!' Mercie called. . . .
'You are wondering what is
wrong with Amanda. She is
trying to bear her own guilt;
that is a burden too heavy for
anyone to carry.'" . . .
. . . "'What will help her?
Will she ever be herself?'
[Hero asked.]
[Mercie answered.] "'The
King can help her. When we
walk through the Sacred
Flames, we always become
what we really are. Amanda
needs to go back to the Great
Celebration. The cure for disobedience is to obey again.'
"Hero thought about his
own unfulfilled vow. 'Is she
afraid of the Sacred Flames?'
he asked.
"The old woman looked at
him. . . . 'You are afraid of the
Sacred Flames. Amanda is
afraid of the King. She is
afraid he will banish her,
because she has been faithless.'
"Mercie looked far away, as
though she was seeing something far off. 'We all have to
walk through what we fear
most in order to gain the
thing we want most. What do
you want most, Hero?'"

Tales of the Kingdom,
David and Karen Mains

145

*M*y Holy of Holies, don't be shocked that I would call you My holy of holies. That's exactly what you are. You are the place of My presence. My law and My power are in you. You have been cleansed by the blood sprinkling. My Shekinah glory burns in you. You are My most holy place. All my shaping and molding is for one purpose: to display My splendor through you, to make you holy on the outside so the inner chamber of My presence will be seen.

✣

"When in the presence of God lowliness of heart has become, not a posture we assume for a time, when we think of Him, or pray to Him, but the very spirit of our life, it will manifest itself in all our bearings towards our brethren. . . . The insignificances of daily life are the importances and tests of eternity, because they prove what really is the spirit that possesses us."

Humility: The Beauty of Holiness,
Andrew Murray

Love the World

"'For God so loved the world that he gave his one and only Son, that whoever believes in him shall not perish but have eternal life'" (John 3:16 NIV).

Father, put Your world on my heart. Cause me to love with Your self-giving passion. Let me see through Your eyes. Teach me how to recognize the pain hidden by pretense, the sorrow disguised by swagger. Move me with the plight of a decaying world—a world for whom You gave all.

Read:
Revelation 14:6
Romans 5:6–8
Luke 19:10

Take time to let the Spirit of God pour the love of God into your
heart.

Savior, I know that I cannot invite You into my life and leave a dying world out. It is through me that You want to reach out, beseech the lost, love the hurting, supply the needy. Until Your agenda is mine, I am not unreservedly surrendered. Make me Yours.

✤

"When you invite
Jesus into your heart,
you'd better make
room for all the
friends He brings
along with Him."

Tommy Tyson

Father, You are everywhere I look. You have transformed my seeing. I am dying to my littleness so that I can live in Your greatness. Now You look out from my eyes and see my world. You look with tenderness and patience and unfathomable love. Little by little, I'm seeing as You see.

❖

"There stands the world
of struggling, sinful,
earth-blinded men and
nations . . . all lapped in
the tender, persuading
Love at the Center. . . .
Marks of glory are upon
all things, and the
marks are cruciform
and blood-stained."

A Testament of Devotion,
Thomas R. Kelly

Gracious One, as You hold me close to Your heart, our hearts are becoming one. In Your presence, my sin-altered priorities are being restored to their eternal position.

✢

"Guidance of life by the Light within . . . begins first of all in a mass revision of our total reaction to the world. Worshipping in the light we become new creatures, making wholly new and astonishing responses to the entire outer setting of life. . . . The dynamic illumination from the deeper level is shed upon the judgments of the surface level, and lo, the 'former things are passed away, behold, they are become new.'

"Paradoxically, this total Instruction proceeds in two opposing directions at once. We are torn loose from the earthly attachments and ambitions. . . . And we are quickened to a divine but painful concern for the world. . . . He plucks the world out of our hearts, loosening the chains of attachment. And He hurls the world into our heart, where we and He together carry it in infinitely tender love."

A Testament of Devotion,
Thomas R. Kelly

Loving Lord, let me be the censer that spreads the aroma of the knowledge of You everywhere. As if I were an alabaster jar filled with priceless perfume, break me. Empty me out at Your feet. Let the fragrance of You fill the world around me.

"The true prophetic message always calls us to stretch our arms out wide and embrace the whole world. In holy boldness we cover the earth with the grace and the mercy of God."

Prayer,
Richard J. Foster

Creator, I give myself unreservedly to You. My body is on Your altar waiting to be consumed by the fire from heaven. I do not belong to myself; I belong to You. Count me among Your treasured possessions. Do through me what You will, when You will, how You will.

✣

"Take your everyday,
ordinary life—your
sleeping, eating,
going-to-work, and
walking-around life—
and place it before
God as an offering."

(Rom. 12:1
The Message)

*W*orld Lover,
You have
my permission to
love Your world
through me any-
time You want.

If I open my heart to
    You
Then I have opened
    my heart to the
    world.

Disturbing thought.

The world may not be
    respectful
Of my schedule
Or the demands on
    my
Energy.
The world may
    clamor for my
    attention
At inconvenient times.

Are there ever
    intervals
When the world
Is not on Your heart?

Perhaps we could
    arrange to meet
Then—
Just the two of us.

"The Inconveniences
of Love,"
Jennifer Kennedy Dean

*God of All
Comfort,
Your perfectly
restored, resurrec-
tion body retained
its wounds. The
hand You stretch
out to the world is
a wounded hand.
Give me the
courage to heal out
of my own wound-
edness. Let me pass
along the miracu-
lous balm that
took the pain out
of my injuries.*

✤

PASSION FOR
COMPASSION
Keep open
to pain
his hers theirs
as well as yours

Threshold
deep wide
for untranquilized
empathizers

Agony
can create capacity
to respond
in kind

Acute heartbreak
walks back
to gather pieces
bandage wounds

Sensitive
to all living
all suffering
let mercy thrive

You! Jonah!
Thomas John Carlisle

All-seeing One, give me x-ray eyes to see through the walls in the lives of my neighbors, my family members, the strangers on my way. Give me grace to envision Your finished work even in its beginning stages.

✢

"[Jesus] stubbornly rejected their surface appearances. He ignored the nicely calculated probabilities of society's judgment of what one might expect of them. He penetrated even the heavy wrappings of what they had themselves settled for in their lives and pierced through to what in their deepest yearnings they still longed to become. He drew this out, confirmed it, and [they] acknowledged it and accepted it. He answered expectantly to that of God in each of them and they felt and responded to the quickening."

On Listening to Another,
Douglas V. Steere

Jennifer Kennedy Dean has become a leader in the study of prayer. Her previous titles include *Heart's Cry* (Principles of Prayer), *The Praying Life: Living Beyond Your Limits,* and *Power Praying: Prayer That Produces Results.* She is also co-founder of the Praying Life Foundation. Through this ministry, Dean conducts international and multidenominational seminars addressing prayer as a relationship rather than an activity. She lives in Blue Springs, Missouri, with her husband, Wayne, and their three sons.